My Old Man Was Always on the Lam

Also by Tony Medina

POETRY

An Onion of Wars
Broke on Ice
Committed to Breathing
Sermons from the Smell of a Carcass Condemned to Begging
No Noose Is Good Noose
Emerge & See

FOR YOUNG READERS

The President Looks Like Me
I and I, Bob Marley
Follow-up Letters to Santa from Kids Who Never Got a Response (YA)
Love to Langston
Christmas Makes Me Think
DeShawn Days

EDITED BY TONY MEDINA

Bum Rush the Page: A Def Poetry Jam (with Louis Reyes Rivera)
Role Call: A Generational Anthology of Social and Political Black Literature & Art
(with Samiya A. Bashir and Quraysh Ali Lansana)
In Defense of Mumia (with S.E. Anderson)

My Old Man Was Always on the Lam

TONY MEDINA

The New York Quarterly Foundation, Inc.
New York, New York

NYQ Books™ is an imprint of The New York Quarterly Foundation, Inc.

The New York Quarterly Foundation, Inc.
P. O. Box 2015
Old Chelsea Station
New York, NY 10113

www.nyqbooks.org

Copyright © 2010 by Tony Medina

All rights reserved. No part of this book may be used or reproduced in any manner whatsoever without written permission of the author.

Second Edition
The First Edition of this book was presented by Nightshade Press.

Set in Gill Sans

Layout and Design by Miriam M. Ahmed | www.miryum.com
Cover Photograph by Adger W. Cowans

Library of Congress Control Number: 2011920124

ISBN: 978-1-935520-36-8

Acknowledgments

Grateful acknowledgment is made to the publishers and editors of the following publications, in which some of the poems in this collection previously appeared: *Committed to Breathing* (Third World Press), "Light"; *Love to Mama* (Lee & Low Books), "My Grandmother Had One Good Coat"; *Family Pictures* (Capital BookFest), "Feeding My Mother at Seventy-two"; *Paterson Literary Review* (Issue Number 37), "I Mainline Heroin" and "Feeding My Mother at Seventy-two"; *Hostos Review* (Issue 2), "My Father Is Hailing a Cab," "My Father Is a Brown Scar," "What's Left of My Father," "I Have Inherited My Father's Things" and "Ward of the State"; *Paterson Literary Review* (Issue Number 32), "My Father Is Hailing a Cab," "My Father Is a Brown Scar," "What's Left of My Father" and "I Have Inherited My Father's Things"; *Harpur Palate* (Volume 2, Number 1), "Ward of the State"; *Connotations Press: An Online Artifact* (Honorée Fanonne Jeffers, Guest Editor), "I Spent the First Years of My Life in the Arms of Firemen" and "Alfie's".

Special thanks are due to the following for their love, support, and insight during the writing of this collection: Maria Mazziotti Gillan, Leslie Heywood and Jennifer Gillan. Thanks to fellow artists and comrades Quraysh Ali Lansana, Nancy D. Tolson, Michelle Holder, Melanie Henderson and Gabrielle David. Thanks to Robert Dugan, Sherry S. Strain, Patricia Jennings and the rest of the crew at Keystone College's Nightshade Press. Thanks to Raymond P. Hammond and The New York Quarterly Foundation, Inc. for reissuing this edition. Thanks also to Adger W. Cowans for the fabulous cover photo of Fannie Lou Hamer's house taken during his sojourn with S.N.C.C. (Student Non-Violence Coordinating Committee) in the 1960s/1970s. And thanks to Miriam Ahmed for the fantastic cover and book design.

I would also like to thank the Clark Foundation, the Newhouse Award and the Binghamton Award at Binghamton University, SUNY, for fellowships and awards that afforded me the time and space to complete this book.

IN MEMORY OF MY MOTHER AND FATHER

**And for Eleanor W. Traylor,
In all her glory**

Contents

My Old Man Was Always on the Lam	1
My Father Is a Matchstick	3
My Father Is Hailing a Cab	4
High Blood Pressure	5
My Father Is a Brown Scar	7
What I Remember Best	8
Hey, Pop!	10
They Wanted Me to Pull the Plug	12
What Do I Do	13
The Great Escape	14
I Don't Want to Remember	16
My heart all mad with misery	18
Going to Your Funeral	20
What's Left of My Father	22
At Saint Raymond's Cemetery	23
The Night We Laid My Father Out	25
After Your Funeral	27
I Have Collected My Father's Things	28
How Do You Pack the House	29
The Week My Father Died	31
I Have Inherited My Father's Things	32
In My Father's Photo Album	33
Hey Pop, Is There Sound Where You Are	34
I Dare You	36
My Father Was the One	37
The Old Folks in Front of My Father's Building	38
How Much Stark Work It Takes to Fend Off Death	39
Ghosts of the Horse	41
Ward of the State	42
My Mother Shows Up in My Life	43
I Was Born on a Saturday Night	46
What Was It Like	47
We Met Brief	48
Light	49

When There Is Nothing Left to Say	50
At 35	52
When I Can't Sleep	54
It's Better Not to Know	55
I Am a Stranger in My Mother's House	56
My Father's Mother Was My Mother	58
The Building on Simpson Street	60
Santeria Saturdays	62
And on Sundays We Went to Church	63
Winter	64
Those Gray Throgs Neck Winter Days	65
As a Kid I Slept on the Top Bunk	66
Second Grade	68
Sunday Morning	69
When I Was a Kid	70
My Grandmother Had One Good Coat	71
Childhood in the Projects Is a Fashion Show Nightmare	72
I Spent the First Years of My Life in the Arms of Firemen	74
Alfie's	75
Autobiography of a Skinny Puerto Rican Kid from the Projects	76
Thanksgiving at Our House	79
Is There Anything in the World Sadder Than	80
36	82
It Is Hard for Me to Think of You	83
I Am Here in the Pathmark among the Cheeses	84
My Mother Who Gasps for Air	86
I Mainline Heroin	87
September	88
Room 102, Bed A	89
Feeding My Mother at Seventy-two	90
Arrival	91
The First and Only Thanksgiving with My Mother	94
The Old Testament	96

Death flickering in you like a pilot light.

—William Mathews

My Old Man Was Always on the Lam

My old man was always on the lam
From love & life from family & me
Ran the streets like they was a

Treadmill & he, Richard Simmons,
Charles Atlas or Jack LaLanne
Ran through women like they was

The Holland Tunnel & he, a little
Red Corvette, a rented limo, a
Taxi with the meter off

My old man was always on
Course to get his mack on or his
Jones on with style for miles

Oh my old man had smarts, my old
Man had pride & integrity, read history
Books & studied society, he could've been a

Preacher a politician or magician
Put a spell on you with disappearing acts
Have you believe a lie was true

My old man I sure did love
As trite as it may sound or seem
As often as he would slide & scheme

My old man was always on the move
A black cat with nine lives
Landing on his feet

Had young girls come
To his funeral discreet
Behind straw hats

TONY MEDINA

Had folks talk about him like he was
Stagolee or Shine, like life was the Titanic
& he was lapping fine

Stroke for stroke
What finally took him out
Maximized on pleasure

Left a hell of a good-looking corpse
My old man, so smooth & fine,
I hated to burn him up

My Father Is a Matchstick

My father is a matchstick
Running through Harlem,

Hailing a cab with a flame
Raging through his head.

His skull is a tulip of fire
Cupping his screaming brain,

Blood bursting from each vessel
Like black ink racing through

The pores of white tissue.
No matter the chatter of teeth

Clenched in agonizing pain,
Nor the arms flopping about

In heavy exhausted hysteria,
Cabs will not stop. He is a black man

In Harlem trying to hail a cab
From the hell unleashed

In his brain, but he can't
Flag one down, they won't

Stop. He stumbles and rests
Along parked cars and meters,

Along sewer holes and debris,
His tongue fumbling around

In his jaw that won't clench
Shut, save for the final stab

And jab, *Ta...x...i! Ta...x...i!*
But as his head rings with pain

And the blood drips through
The brain like an IV bag dripping

Drops of water like torture,
No one will stop, no one will

Stop

TONY MEDINA

My Father Is Hailing a Cab

My father is hailing a cab
In Harlem

Not to his initial destination,
The place he was planning to go

With a bottle of wine
And freshly shined shoes

With his suit & tie and
Old Spice slapped on

His freshly shaved face

His pressure is too high
It shoots up through the roof

Of his head, catching him
Off guard,

Stroke for stroke,
Like a terrorist attack

He goes down like a building
Hit by planes, collapsing

In place, a slump
Of shoulder, an arm

Gone dead, the prickly
Itch of blood

Stunned beneath a
Heavy veil of flesh

High Blood Pressure

In the belly
Of your brain

Blood hot silent
Eruption

Of salt & rage
68 years

Of *tecata* screams
68 years

Of street hustle
Schemes

Your mother
Weeps

By the window
Black rosary beads

Faded by sweat
& worry

The body pincushioned
Into stab marks

Stitched together
By concrete

& tar of shitty
Harlem streets

Prison cells are fat
With our flesh

Spit us out like
Vomit of a child

One spoonful
At a time

The life you live
You do not own

Do not waste it
Breaking mirrors

The cracks show up
Inside your skull

The brain is an egg yolk
Stabbed with toast

The hard sharp edge of life
Lived on the edge of corners

Lived on the out
Skirts & curbs

Oh do not help them
Push you off

A pigeon with
No wings

Beneath the tires
Of a cross-town bus

Flying feathers and
Blood and dust

68 years
Of ashes to ashes

& dust to dust

Shards show up
Inside your skull

Oh do not help them
Push you off

My Father Is a Brown Scar

My father is a brown scar
On a white bedspread,
A pincushion stapled
Together with needles,
A slab of flesh
With tubes going
Through him like
Turnpikes, driven
To this last bed
By a brain that
Popped like an
Egg. His nails
Are immaculately
Kept, his arms
Map out his
Dumb youthful
Wasteful trackmark
Days full of arrogance
Confusion and rage.
My father is a beanbag
Slumped in a corner,
His mouth wrenched open
To receive holy communion
From the world of medicine
And science, the world
Of mechanical breathing
And silence. My father
Looks good looks boyish
In his white hair and
Overnight shadow.
My father is a brown dot
In a sea of infinite white space.
My father is a memory I wear
On my face.

What I Remember Best

Clenching my teeth in a yellow cab
Stuck on the Brooklyn Bridge
Clenching my teeth in the mouth
Of all that traffic and noise, drivers
Banging their dashboards,
Honking horns and cursing
And me in the back of that cab in the
Middle of the day, the sun as pale as the cab

I'm melting in the vinyl seat cushions
From what I gathered on the phone
At Samiya's—My aunt's voice
Came on the machine after the beep,
Solemn and stuttering:
> *Your father's in the hospital…*
> *It doesn't look too good—*
> *Come as soon as you can.*

What I remember best is running
Out into the streets of Park Slope, Brooklyn,
Frantically hailing a cab—stuck for half-an-hour
In an uptown traffic jam, the radio
Blaring baseball scores, weather reports and salsa
And me in the backseat trying not to sob and
Panic and me in the backseat
Wanting to disappear, to wake up

In my bed in Harlem to find that this
Was only a dream, that my aunts and uncle
Were not in the ICU at St. Vincent's,
That my old man wasn't a few feet
Away unconscious in the next room

What I remember best is clenching my teeth
As the doctor held up the X-rays of
My father's brain, *There's not much*
    We can do—As you can see blood is everywhere…
    It's up to you what you want us to do.

Clenching my teeth in the ICU
My aunts and uncle
Waiting around, silent
And me, alone in that room,
Not knowing what to do.

Hey, Pop!

You left so suddenly
Your head just popped

Like a sunny-side up egg
Stabbed with toast

At 68 you still ran the streets
Like you were 20 or 30 or 45

Half your life spent slinging
Scag and shooting smack,

That long stretch in the joint,
The scar across your torso

Still dark and visible
Like the brandished bronze

Of a whip and just like
The snap & whirl

Of a whip you turned
Your whole life around

From prison to culinary school
From addict to rehab group

And drug counselor—
Going to college in your sixties!

Hey, Pop!
You left so soon

I never even had
A chance to show you

The book I dedicated
To you

I was stuck in a cab
In Brooklyn trying to get

Across the Manhattan Bridge
Into the Village

To see you laid up
In some hospital bed

At St. Vincent's
How peaceful you looked

As if you were dreaming
I couldn't take you

Lying there with tubes
Running through your

Flesh, a machine
Breathing for you

The doctor said
The blood was everywhere

They wanted me to
Make the decision

Not to resuscitate,
But I said *No*,

I said *Fuck that* and
Held out for some hope—

Your skinny communist kid
Praying for a miracle

They Wanted Me to Pull the Plug

As you lay there serene
In your frozen slumber

Wanted me wanted me
To pull your plug, end

Your life after you
Drove yourself to

The emergency room
From Harlem

A last wild effort
To fight for your

Life, a few more moments
Of dreams and frantic

Breathing, wanted me,
Wanted me, your second

Born son, second to hold
Your name, to make

The decision to
Pull the plug and keep

Your lungs from breathing,
Keep your heart from

Beating, since your dreams
Were drowning in a bone

Shell of porridge, your brain
Turning to mush, but I

Did not have the will
Or courage

What Do I Do

After your brain splits

Like a grape, like an overripe
Tomato in a Harlem sun

Blood spilling out
Like ink on paper,

The doctor holding up the X-ray
Like a Rorschach test

*As you can see
Blood is everywhere*, he says

As I stare at the
Brown scar of you

Slouched stiff
On a white sheet

Like a broom,
Your mouth tight as a

Fist around
A tube,

A machine holding up
Your lungs

What do I do,
Pop

With your brain
Half dead

And you barely
In this room

*As you can see
As you can see*

And the doctor said
And the doctor says

You won't make it
Through

The Great Escape

There are so many ways
So many ways to die

Laid up in the ICU
With your mouth

Twisted open & a tube
Down your throat

So many ways so many ways
The brain bursts into

Red molten wax
Your body slumped in a

Corner like a throw rug
So many ways so many ways

To slip into a coma slip
Out of your own body

Your breathing
Suddenly arrested

Your pulse slipped
From its veins

So many ways
For your bones

To collapse
Like a steeple

Of playing cards
The lungs trapped

In its delicate cage
So many ways

So many ways
For the heart

To escape
Into its web

Of blood & dust
So many ways so many

Ways to slip out with
Your head on fire

I Don't Want to Remember

The last time my father spoke to me
Through answering machine
Cursing about some thing or other

How I wanted to go through the
Phone and grab him by the throat
Didn't he know I was busy

Didn't he know I had my own life
That my time was limited
Didn't he know that at 35

To hear *Motherfucker* aimed
At me from someone
Who never cursed at me
Would drive me to rage—
To shut him out completely

I don't want to remember
That my old man was old
And facing death so sudden

That he, at 68, with a growing
Reluctance to climb stairs and try
To catch his breath

With bouts of depression
Masked by talk of politics
And a quick hearty laugh
Was facing his last days

I don't want to remember
The guilt I felt for not having
Visited him more, for not allowing him
Into my life fully, never making the time

To hang out and shoot the shit,
To show him the book
I dedicated to him,
To listen to his plans

I don't want to remember
That I, at 35, so far removed
From the life my father chose,

Had finally stepped into his shoes
Never available, never there
Too busy for my own good

My heart all mad with misery,

My old man laid up on a white bedspread, tubes going through him like turnpikes. He caught a cab from Harlem to St. Vincent's Hospital in the Village. His head was on fire, the Old Spice flaring up with sweat. His hot date had taken a turn for the worse. It would not be with the woman of his dreams, but of his nightmare. He left a bottle of wine on top of the fridge, a tightly rolled joint hidden in his desk on some jazz tapes. When I got to the hospital, he was already in a coma. The nurse said he'd been laying up in the emergency room for three days. No one in the family had received a call. God knows what could've happened to him those three nights his brain leaked like a tire. The last time I saw him we were at Mickey D's on 117th Street. He suddenly upped and split, in the middle of a conversation, as if a heavy cloud had sat on his shoulders. *What's the matter? Where are you going?* I remember asking him as he walked up the block toward his apartment. *I don't know. I just got these feelings. I'll be alright. We'll talk, I'll see you soon.* And just like that he was gone. The time before that I noticed how he'd lose his breath climbing the stairs to my second floor apartment. It startled me to see him pause at the first landing. Even though he was 68 with white hair and mustache, he had a baby face. He looked 48 and swam every other day at the Y, walked from the Bronx to Harlem to Midtown and the Lower East Side and back. I remember as a child how he used to take me to the Reservoir to run laps. He's the reason I became a vegetarian. Ever since he got high blood pressure and kicked heroin, he'd been on a health and exercise kick, so much so I began to check him out and look at other people in our family, how they'd let themselves go, eat everything, all day in front of the TV. Every time we'd get together for holidays, the kids would get bigger and bigger to where I could not recognize them. But it was my old man, watching him throughout the years, how he did yoga and swam and walked and ate lentil beans and brown rice, fresh green salads and on and on that got me worried about what I put into my body.

Seeing him in that hospital bed, how peaceful he looked, yet his mouth wrenched open to a point of confusion, the tube in his mouth forcing a perplexed looked, as if his face was shoved into a question mark to say, *Is this it? Is this how it all ends? I don't even get a chance to get my shit together and go out with some dignity?*

Going to Your Funeral

With your boombox
On my lap and a bag

Full of Sarah Vaughn
And Barry White CDs

Rolling through your
Stomping grounds in a cab

Passing by the shoppers
On 116th Street

The methadone addicts
On 125th & Lex

Pincushioned abandoned buildings
Of flesh

I'm thinking of John Coltrane's
Love Supreme

How sorrow climbs
Out of his horn

Like the sun
Or Billie Holiday

Tearing out her soul
As if her skin were a dress,

The red raw fruit of *her* pain—
Trackmarks on her heart—

As we hunch up onto the
FDR Drive on our way

To your funeral
Where you wait

Impatiently
In a steel rented box

With your boyish face
With the thick white mustache

Your blue mismatched suit
How brown and beautiful

And suave you are
Even in death

What's Left of My Father

Is in a charcoal box my shoes
Can't fit in. I think to myself,
He was short, but not that short!

I carried him in my lap from the funeral
Home to St. Raymond's Cemetery
Where his mother and father
And brothers are buried.

People were going about
Their business as if nothing mattered
But their lives, their feelings.

In the backseat of my aunt's car, I
Sank into the seat cushions
Like loose change or pocket lint
Thinking about my father

With his five-foot four inch smile,
His big laugh and baby face
With the thick white mustache.

How could all that life be smashed
Down into something the size of a
Sugar container?

Inside the car, my aunts remained silent,
Letting me brood, letting me take it all in,
Deal with the fact that my father left no
Money to bury him; that against my wishes,

Against my fears, not his, I was forced to
Cremate him, burn that beautiful brown face
I've known all my life.

At Saint Raymond's Cemetery

My aunts waited for me
To pick up my father's

Ashes from the funeral
Home. The mortician

Handed me a box with
His ashes and had me

Sign for it; cold and
Clinical and with a

Price tag, my father had
Been put in his place.

We drove to St. Raymond's
Cemetery where most

Of our family is buried. My
Grandfather, who I barely

Knew because he died when
I was a baby; my grandmother,

Who raised me, kept me from
Being a ward of the state, a year

Into foster care, a year after
My mother left me in the

Hospital to get high after she
Gave birth; my uncles Robert,

Raymond and Ralphie, all
Died young, died too soon.

We took a couple of makeshift
Shovels and dug up the topsoil

Of my grandmother's grave
And placed the plastic, shoebox-

Sized poor man's urn with my
Father's ashes, covered it

And said a prayer.
And just like that

My father was put
In his place

The Night We Laid My Father Out

The night we laid my father out
People came to the Bronx from all over:

Family and friends, long-lost relatives
And mystery women all showed up—

Some unexpectedly; there had been
No formal plans, no one knew

What to do, or expect. My father
Wasn't religious, so we didn't plan

On having a holy man come and
Give a prayer. But my aunts,

His sisters, were uneasy about sending
Their brother off without a formal

Blessing. As people came and left the viewing
Room as they wished, Sarah Vaughn and

Billie Holiday sang from the belly
Of his boombox that stood at the

Foot of the steel-gray rent-a-coffin;
Nieces and nephews cried, ate junk food,

Drank soda, gossiped, bullshitted
And mourned like it was a holiday

Get together. I finally flagged a priest
From a funeral next door. And after

Agreeing to do the Hail Marys for
A few bucks, he sent my father off to

The hereafter all clean and spiffy for God
And my aunts. Then my uncle broke the ice

By having everyone tell stories. One by
One people from all over came up to speak:

People who knew him in another life,
Another light: Coworkers and clients

He counseled, family members he touched,
Folks who never spoke in public before,

Began telling stories and jokes until the night
Turned into a roast. One of his coworkers from

The drug rehab facility he worked at
On Roosevelt Island in Queens, a younger

Cat with dreadlocks, talked about the time
My father was doing a headstand yoga position

On the lawn in the middle of Marcus Garvey Park
In Harlem. He said a couple of teenagers from

The neighborhood came up to my father and said,
Mister, don't you think you're a little too old

To be break dancing? Instead of tear-jerking eulogies,

Aunts and uncles and cousins and
Friends alike started doing stand-up routines

About my old man. We ended the night
By talking about how much of a lady's man

He was, how he left because Clinton moved in,
And there was only room for one mack in Harlem,

While Barry White sang, *Ec sta cy...when you
Lay down next to me...*

After Your Funeral

Carefully rummaging
Through your things

The gravity of that room
The heat and silence

My head strained
By a numb sadness

Moving about
Mechanically

I stood in the center
Surveying the sudden

Sad disruption
Of a life interrupted

Dust and dead roaches
Cobwebs and a finely rolled joint

Hidden among jazz tapes
And salsa, the music

That held you together

I sat there
Like a crash test dummy

In the wreckage
Of your life

Not knowing
Where to begin

I Have Collected My Father's Things

I have collected my father's things
After the sudden wake and quick cremation
Collected what spare remains he left behind
Like the bone fragments and ash spit up
By the flames of the crematorium
That claimed his cold flesh

How we become our mother and father
From what they leave us: words images
Ideas and expressions, books & records
& useless sentimental knickknacks,
The random fragments of life as they lived it
From moment to moment

How we discover things about them
We never knew

Pop, I didn't want to burn your body
To bone bits and ash. I didn't want to
Put you in a skimpy box a pair of shoes
Could not fit in. I did not want to leave you
Beneath the topsoil of your mother's grave
For some random crank to discover and discard

Even though that's what you always
Wanted

How Do You Pack the House

How do you pack the house
Of your life or someone

You love what do
You do with it all

Those things tied to
Someone else's memory

And you tied to them
How do you throw your

Dead father's clothes away,
Find a place for his books

And papers what do you
Do with all the unwanted

Sentimental things that clutter
His desk and drawers

That meant something
To him from moment to

Moment year to year
Do you burn them away

In your memory like
Your old man in a

Slaty five-inch plastic box
Do you throw them

Out with yesterday's trash
Or find a place at the bottom

Of your closet and lug them
Around from moment

To moment year to year
Do you carry them

Around with you from year
To year out of guilt or fear

How do you pack the house
Of your life or someone

You love

The Week My Father Died

The week my father died my sister called out of the blue, after fifteen years. I remember speaking to her on a payphone from the lobby of the visitor's area of the ICU at St. Vincent's. My father was a few yards away slumped on a hospital bed with tubes going through him and a machine for breathing. He was not her father, but she loved him just the same; and had to pull over on a street in New Haven before jumping the curb, careening into a streetlight or telephone pole with a cell phone in her hand.

Whenever she calls I get a sudden nervous lump in my gut where others would probably be elated. She, on the other hand, is overwhelmed to hear my voice and equally overwhelms me with news of my long-absent mother, missing from the maternity ward after giving birth to me.

I know that she's in a desperate way, not for money or shelter, but to connect me to our mother, to re-connect me to her who was born in prison to a mother hooked on heroin and raised in a sort of prison in a Puerto Rican family that thought they were white and let her know how black she was every chance they got.

Till this day those scars stick to her like the DNA that formed her beautiful full lips and thick black hair and red brown cocoa face.

She didn't call to tell me about her new kid or the newborn she lost to a drug dealer boyfriend who, mishandling his loaded gun, sent a bullet into his soft, underdeveloped newborn skull; or her stints in rehab or AA, but to connect her with her mother who shut her out of her life, unable to deal with her accusations and pain.

I Have Inherited My Father's Things

I have inherited my father's things
His bed his couch his radio and TV
Boxes of books bags of clothes
Pots & pans and dishes, knickknacks
And other sentimental useless things

Which makes it hard to move about
My apartment, since it's the size
Of a quarter; it's so small as soon as
You walk in the front door, you fall
Out the window

My aunts say I should get rid of his things
Give his clothes to a church or the Salvation
Army; but I keep picturing him in his place
With his things, moving about in his blue
Robe and slippers

I have inherited my father's things
His bed slouches against a wall in my
Hall, his clothes are roadblocks in
My living room

My aunts say I shouldn't burden myself,
But I keep picturing him in that hospital bed
With a tube in his mouth and his lungs
Tied to a machine

I imagine him in a cab on his way to
The emergency room with the inside
Of his head on fire

I have inherited my father's things
His birth certificate and credit cards
His awards and plaques and papers
Of accomplishment,

His driver's license and photo album
Pictures of him forever staring back at me

In My Father's Photo Album

There are pictures of him
When he was my age & younger

In some of them he looks like
Someone out of *The Battle of Algiers*

Posing with his prison buddies
Posing with his rehab group

With various women he had
Throughout his Rico Suavé life—

My mother on a Brooklyn beach,
Sun-tanned with jet-black hair

In a one-piece; my brother's mother,
Sarah, the love of his life, her smooth

Brown regal beauty towering
Over him—

From Harlem to the Bronx to
Chi-Town to Harlem

Mapping out a life of second
Guesses & second chances

Brown man poor man short man
Skinny man Black man Puerto Rican

His quick adulthood of low self-esteem
& street hustle schemes &

Sax man Birdland dreams
Wore out too soon

In the photos you could see it in his eyes
Peeling through the laughter

The light & glimmer of someone fumbling
Against his own restlessness & confusion

Hey Pop,
Is There Sound Where You Are

What melody is played
To tap your heart

And set your mind
At ease

Or rain dancing
About your head

Like piano keys

Sometimes when I'm
Alone

I picture you in that
Grim rented box

In your mix-
Matched suit with

Your smooth
Brown face and

Manicured hands
Calm and serene

As yellow leaves
Not in a million years

Would I have pictured
You there in that metallic

Box we rented
For that final night

And fateful day
They shipped you

Off to the crematorium
To come back to me

In a pale plastic
Shoebox of bone & ash

Hey, Pop
Is there sound

Where you are
What melody is played

What memory of you
Will last

I Dare You

Was the first book I ever owned.

    It was one of those self-help inspirational

Books they give you in prison or rehab.

    My father sprang it on me one day

When I was ten. I tried reading it

    A thousand times but couldn't get

Into it. I blamed it on a steady diet

    Of TV & no one besides him

To push books on me. Even after

    Years later when books were my fix

& I could never get enough, I

    Could never go back to that little

Burgundy hardback my father

    Gave me that helped him see life

Differently & see himself on the other side

    Of the curb on the other side of a

Prison cell to stand & be his own man.

    Till this day I wonder what he was

Trying to say by teaching me to play chess

    & giving me that little book.

My Father Was the One

My father was the one
Who taught me how
To drive in the parking lot

Of the old folks home
Where I'd chase down
Old ladies in their walkers,

Dentures flying in the air,
Swerving around
Devil-may-care

He'd scream
Stop the car! Stop the car!
Put it in reverse!

My father was the one
Who taught me to drive
A hearse with a cold corpse

Supine in the rear and
Johnny Mathis lullabies
In my ear

He was a dear, my father
Was; he'd say, *Here*
Have a beer

As I swung the hearse
Around that narrow
Parking lot taunting the

Old women with their loose
Teeth and varicose knots
Lifting up their canes

Like middle fingers

The Old Folks
in Front of My Father's Building

The old folks
   In front
      Of my father's
Building are
   Buildings that
      Have been
Abandoned
   They sit
      On broken
Benches
   Watching
      The dirty
Pigeons
   Strut and
      Peck &
Taunt the
   Ancient
      Statues
Of flesh dry &
   Flabby in the
      Wind

The old folks
   In front
      Of my father's
Building are
   Gray in
      A gray
Landscape
   Even when
      The sun is
Splashed
   Yellow like
      Van Gogh's
Sunflowers
   Thick &
      Heavy on a
Gloomy
   Harlem
      Canvas
Of old age
   Concrete &
      Sorrow

How Much Stark Work It Takes to Fend Off Death*

To try & get
   Away

From it
   By hailing

A cab
   Though your head

Is on fire
   & your right side

Collapses in place
   Like a building

Hit by a plane
   A fly stunned

In mid arc
   An old damp porch

Slumped in exasperation
   Giving in to the blue-gray

Sadness of gravity & time
   Suddenly gone by

What you always knew
   & expected

What you secretly feared
   & accepted

How much work
   It takes

To keep death
   At bay

To pacify it
   Like a lion tamer

TONY MEDINA

By throwing peanuts
    & chairs & frustrated

Fits of rage
    Trying to beat

Its breath back
    Trying to keep

Its teeth
    From grinding

You up
    In its big black

Awful mouth
    As if it somehow

Got loose
    From its cage

Your arm too heavy
    To lift

Your tongue too fat
    To sift the words

Out of your
    Wrung-shut mouth

Trying to get
    Your breath

Back enough
    To say

Taxi…
    Taxi

*William Mathews

Ghosts of the Horse

My father coaxes my mother to Chi-Town
The lure of easy money making salads
At a hotel. My mother can't turn it down
With a daughter to feed, a habit to rid

But my father is being a man, the kind
Who expects sex in exchange for dinner
My mother's changed, she's back in her right mind
My father tries to push the issue further

He can't manhandle and manipulate her
Like his pimp days using her to feed his fix
Those numbed memories come rushing back to her
Ghosts of the horse coursing through her veins for kicks

She leaves her suitcase and everything behind
She wishes she could take her life and rewind

Ward of the State

Your father is running the streets
Your mother is hiding in abandoned buildings
The two of them are mainlining their way out of your life
The world is a room the color of a filing cabinet
Strange hands have dragged you kicking & screaming
From your mother's womb
Her hands will not hold you
Her eyes will turn away
Strange hands will have to do for now,
Placing you in an incubator or state-issued basinet
Your chest is caved in
You weigh less than a cup of snot & tears
Your lungs are a pack of Pall Malls strung together
With shoestring and Krazy Glue,
Thick rubbery phlegm clogging your bronchioles
Soon you will be alone in that room
Until the nurse comes and calls for help
Until the authorities come to take you away
Your first few days will be spent atop a judge's bench
Staring at a yellow bulb drowning in a gray ceiling

Your father is running the streets
Your mother is hiding in abandoned buildings
The two of them don't mean to but are
Mainlining their way out of your life
The world is a room the color of a filing cabinet
You weigh less than a broom
Strange hands will hold you,
Welcome you to your life

My Mother Shows Up in My Life

My mother shows up in my life
As frequently as a meteorite
Burning its way across the sky
Burying its flaming rage
At my doorstep.

My first memory of her
Was when I was four or five
And she visited me on Simpson Street
In the South Bronx.

I remember her taking me
To Woolworth's, and me
Like a spoiled kid just introduced
To Santa Claus, was asking her
For practically everything
In the store.

I remember that night around Christmas
Not because I was with a mother
I barely knew, all dressed in black
And beautiful as if she were on her way
To a funeral or a movie premier
But because it was the first time
I ever got lost

And how panicked she had become,
The first chance she got to make
Things right, reintroduce herself
Into my life after having left me
In the maternity ward at Morrisania Hospital
That January night her jones came down.

If I would have lost you,
Your grandmother would've never
Let me hear the end of it,
She'd say throughout the years
She sporadically popped up
Out of nowhere.

TONY MEDINA

One night around Christmas
She showed up in the tiny
Three-room apartment
My grandmother aunts and
Uncles shared in the projects
In Throgs Neck.

One of my aunts said,
This is your mother,
As she showed up in her black dress
And black hair, tan and beautiful as ever
In the middle of the winter
With a green bike with training wheels.

In my father's photo album
There is a picture of us
In front of a fat Christmas tree.
She with her black dress
And sly Madame smile
And me on that green bike,
Sucking my teeth and
Making faces with my
Flip Wilson Geraldine
Sock-it-to-me impersonation.

After that Christmas Eve
She'd show up every now and then
To take me for weekend trips
To her place on Flatbush Avenue
In Brooklyn, or to Shea Stadium
To see the Mets or to the Statue
Of Liberty where I'm posing
With brown shorts and a light green
Fonzie T-shirt, sticking my thumbs
Out to say, *Aye*—

And after that eleven years
Raced by and she showed up
To my apartment in El Paso
To the home of a married
Military man so far removed
From the baby she left long ago
In that South Bronx hospital room.

It turned out she had friends
In El Paso who invited us to
A party. At the party, my mother
Got embarrassingly drunk,
Berating and belligerent,
Paranoid and apologetic,
Sorry for the years she lost,
The life she lived—leaving me
In the hospital, giving birth
To my sister in prison.

She resented herself
And my grandmother
For not allowing her
To have me back.
She resented the time she lost,
The years she could never get back.
Before she could clash with my wife,
Cooking and cleaning and washing
The dishes, trying to get *her* to mother *me*,
I drove her to the tiny airport in El Paso,
Never to see her again until the next time
My constellation is interrupted
By the scattered burning rocks
Of her pain and regret.

I Was Born on a Saturday Night

My mother drops me from her womb
Like a bad habit, as if to regurgitate.

I leave a bad taste in her mouth,
Leak out like a red drop on white cotton

Drawers, her first menses, stale warm
Water from her ear, as if emerged from

A swim or a shower.
I lie in the maternity ward a wet raisin

Soaked in blood & feces high on
Heroin and Marlboro cigarettes

High on beer & wine & saturated foods,
Unable to scream cry or wince.

My mother is nervous, she is freaking out,
Her womb pulling at her ribs like cobwebs.

My mother can't take it, can't take me,
She has to get up, get out, stick a needle

In her thigh.
I am a dry prune, hairless in a basinet,

A purple blue dot in a pale green hospital room.
My mother jumps up, covers her open

Wailing womb, refuses to look at me
Writhing there like hairballs & dust

On a wicker broom, puts on her coat
Over her gown & with her yellow smiley face

Disposable foam hospital slippers
Runs through the shitty snowy streets

Of the South Bronx off to get her
Saturday night special.

What Was It Like

Those cold January nights after having given
    In to fear & desperation & despair

After having left your second born—me—as soon
    As I slipped from you

My lungs wrapped around the smoke you
    Breathed wrapped around the hot liquid

Rush of scag shot out from dirty needles
    Into your pale arm & thigh

Did you hide out in abandoned buildings
    Strapping your arm with a rubber hose

Or the belt from your hospital gown
    Slapping your vein slapping your vein

Did that vein resemble me—
    Yellow green & swollen

Staring up at you as you turned away
    The needle sinking deeper & deeper

Into your guilt & pain
    Deeper & deeper into your

Desperate shame pulling up pulling
    Out unwanted blood from you

TONY MEDINA

We Met Brief

You did not
Give birth to
Me in pri
Son

Leave me stran
Ded in a ma
Ternity ward in
Cu ba ting

You scraped me
From your you
To rest

Along
The stiff cold
Wire like a hang
Er on

What remained
Of me from you
Still won
Ders why

    Why

Light

It was there where the eyes
Are first exposed to light
Where you learned to adjust them
Those first few waking hours
Where you come out into the world
Kicking and screaming,
Only you did not kick,
Or scream—just wondered
Even at that pale age—
When almost nothing has been
Etched upon the brain, but pain—
That you learn to adjust your eyes
To the light that quickly replaces
The space your mother occupied
When her eyes tried to avoid yours
As the nurse lifted you to her chest,
Wondering why the light was so sharp
And stabbing, the room emptier,
And if your mother
Would ever come back
To claim you

When There Is Nothing Left to Say

When there is nothing left
To say among strangers

Trying to patch their lives
Together through time &

Telephone wire, trying to
Recover the loose strands

And scraps of a relationship
That barely existed

The strange, strained feeling
Of not knowing what to say

To the woman on the other
End of the line who calls

You son & you without
Cause to call her mother

Not knowing what to say
After eleven year gaps

Broken up by days
Too brief to remember

There was a tiny brown boy
You left in the hospital,

His lungs wracked
With the cobwebs of asthma

His blood bitter with
The bile you boiled

On a cooker, off to
Get your fix

Hours after giving
Birth

The needle stitching
A patchwork quilt

Of absence & pain
A lifetime of holes

Larger than all
You cannot recall

At 35

I hardly know my mother
Who left me in the maternity

Ward at Morrisania Hospital
In the South Bronx

January 10th 1966

Gone to chase a fix
Gone to get herself fixed

Leaving you
Was the worse

Thing I ever
Did
        She says

  Till this day
  This day

What deep regrets
She carries

What heavy
Aching pain

To live a life

Without the one
She made & carried

I never hated her
All these days

Never cursed or
      Wished her harm

But felt, instead,
The guilt
And worry

That one day
She'll really

   Be gone

When I Can't Sleep

When I can't sleep, I worry about what was hidden in my house, how we were taught to keep secrets. Like I never knew I was abandoned in the hospital until I was well into my twenties, or that three of my uncles died of AIDS. Recently, my mother reappeared in my life; she resurfaced in Port Richey, Florida, with a house and new husband. Well into her sixties, she retired from Walmart and, in addition to a modest pension, she received a triple bypass. My sister, who she doesn't speak to, who will never forgive her for giving birth to her in prison, for leaving her with a white Puerto Rican family who let her know she was black every chance they got, has been the silent go-between linking me with our mother.

When I finally get up the nerve to call her, after twenty-four years divided by a five-day visit, it was the New Year's after my father died. Her husband, who had been screening her calls from my sister perhaps, from excitement, warned me not to deliver her any bad news, that her heart couldn't take it.

When I finally spoke to her, she said it was the best present she had ever received. She couldn't believe that after all these years, I'd still want to speak to her. When she asked how I got her number, and I told her it was my sister, her daughter, she went silent and quickly changed the subject. Then asked, "How is your father?" Then my end went silent, until I got up the nerve to say, "Oh, he's alright; you know how he is…"

When I can't sleep, I worry about what is hidden in my life; how easy it is to keep secrets; how silence is measured by distance and how with time, my mother, my sister and I drift from one another like strangers with nothing more to share but little white lies and small talk.

It's Better Not to Know

What my mother could not
Bear to tell the night
She left me with the nurse
At Morrisania Hospital

How she couldn't escape
Her jones long enough
To keep me

How I split through
Her aching bones
With weak asthmatic lungs
Determined to breathe

Too young to think
Too young to speak
Where did she go
Where did she go

It's better not to know
The pain she must have gone through
That night her body failed her
With one false move

How she must have regretted
Not being able to get me
Back that first year
I spent in foster care

How she'll carry the empty space
Between us to her grave
How she sacrificed one form of pain
For another longer lasting one

Looking back some thirty-odd years later
I'm left to piece our would-be lives together
With more questions than lies
With less fact than truth

What I feel is not bitterness or
Rage or self-destructive indulgence
But a sorrow as wide as
The void between us

I Am a Stranger in My Mother's House

I am a stranger
    In my mother's house
        I can count the times
We saw each other
    On one hand
        I am a stranger
In my mother's heart
    The last time she
        Saw me
She was drunk
    With guilt
        Lashing out at
My father
    & my
        Grandmother
& her
    Fucked-up life
        I am a stranger
In my mother's house
    Her calls come in
        Eleven-year intervals
The first thing
    She says to me
        After years
Of disappearances is
    How is your father?
        I know she'd had
Triple bypass
    & don't want
        To tell her
That my father
    Had a stroke
        On the streets
Of Harlem
    That he took
        Himself to
The hospital
    In a cab
        & never came

> Back from his coma
>   Instead I say
>   *Oh, he's alright*
> You know how he is…
>   I am a stranger
>   In my mother's house
> An unwanted knot
>   In the memory
>   Of her heart

My Father's Mother Was My Mother

My father's mother was my mother
Not in the *Jerry Springer Ricki Lake*
Salacious dysfunctional family way
But in the way it be
Sometimes when your moms
Runs out on you, leaves
You in the maternity ward
With your pops nowhere
To be found

My father's mother was my mother
She didn't get me at the lost & found
Or at her doorstep 'cause my moms
& pops skipped town
She wrestled me from the metallic
Green arms of the state
A whole year after I was born
As if I were docket number
One hundred and ten

My father's mother was my mother
& the white couple from Queens
Who wanted to be my father & mother
Had to give me over to her

This ain't no tragic mulatto story
Of the black spic baby
With a moms with her jones
Coming down & a pops
In the can on a seven
Year bid

This ain't no *Daddy Was a Numbers Runner*
Down These Mean Streets Manchild
In the Promised Land Seven Long Times
Story

This is about my father's mother
Who was my mother
My Last of the Big Mamas mama
My ace boon coon
Protector & friend
With her own nine children
& her children's children

This is about what some women
Have always done
What they continue to do
How they sacrifice
& defend

The Building on Simpson Street

The building on Simpson Street
Where I grew up is no longer there

I remember the elevated train tracks
A few blocks away, roaring through
My mind like the black plastic wheels
Of my Big Wheel rumbling along

The rough tongue of the sidewalk
Immaculately swept by the super
And splashed in summer sun

The building on Simpson Street
Is where my grandmother leaned
Her brown flabby arms on the
Window ledge, her beautiful black
Rusty elbows bent in prayer

The building on Simpson Street
Where I grew up is where
I caught my cousin
Dry humping a boy behind

The stairs, where my next-door
Neighbor mooned me, flashing
My startled five-year old eyes
With the crack of her ass

The building on Simpson Street
Where I grew up is where so many
Of my relatives lived we had a bed
In the middle of the kitchen

One night we found ourselves
All huddled on it like a tiny island
Frantically trying to kill a rat
The size of a cat with a broom

We had so many fires in that little
Walk-up, seesawing from floor to floor
Fires started by uncles who fell asleep
With lit joints or cigarettes

On summer nights we'd cordon off
The street and roast hot dogs and
Marshmallows in a South Bronx
Bonfire of happiness and love

We never knew we were poor
That moving up in the world
Meant moving into the projects

I always wonder about the
Tenement of my youth
The morning I woke
To the sun pressed warm
Against my skin

To the sound of garbage trucks
And my grandmother
By the window
With her black rosary beads

Silently praying

Santeria Saturdays

We were exiled
   To the back room
Where all the coats
   Were piled on my
Grandmother's bed
   While the grown-ups
Sat around the feast
   In a circle before
The altar, a long table
   Decorated with food
And flowers with
   Candles and holy
Water for the saints
   And for the dead.
My aunt would
   Get possessed,
Take a deep pull
   From a cigar, suck
Back a mouth
   Full of rum, spray
It, then blow smoke
   In the saint's face,
Talking in tongues.
   We'd sneak to the
Living room, nose
   Our way between
Calves and shoes
   Watching in amuse-
Ment at the weird
   Holy sacredness
Of it all, even if
   We did not quite
Know what was
   Going on, knowing
It had something
   To do with Africa,
Puerto Rico, power
   And the spirits,
Always the spirits.

And on Sundays We Went to Church

For our Hail Marys Full of Grace.
We'd sit there before the padded pews
    Gawking up at the majestic murals
& ceiling art of white saints &
Angels soft & round & fluffy as clouds.

We'd trace our eyes along the stained glass
Windows & God's Light shining through
    Like an all-seeing eye trying to catch us
Nodding off & yawning
As the hazy rhythmic drone of the priest's

Prayers & instructions lulled us to
Sleep. We'd struggle & strain to stay
    Awake, pay attention or risk going to
Hell—or worse—have our aunts smack our hand
Our uncles smack us on the back of the

Head or another cousin deliberately yanking
Our shirtsleeves, pinching us awake.
    We waited in excitement for the moment
We'd get to get in line for our wafer & sip
Of wine: The body & blood of Christ,

Amen, making us feel special, feel grown-up,
Then pay ten cents to light a candle
    & wish for money or pray our grand-
Mother got better or our aunt would
Hit the number from the dreams we had the night

Before. But before that, we'd enter the church, do
The sign of the cross, kiss our finger
    Up to God & put holy water on our
Forehead for good luck, to ward off
Evil spirits, remembering to put our crisp, brand new

    Dollar into the collection plate
    During intermission.

TONY MEDINA

Winter

& the skinny
Projects trees
Stick out of the imported
Soil & concrete like
Popsicle sticks
Outside my window

Winter
& the leaves
Are stripped from
Their bony branches
Making the trees look
Like scarecrows
Outside my window

Winter
& the wind that whips
Its way between the buildings
Whistles through my ribcage & lungs
Like cobwebs when I
Jump on the bed to stare
Outside my window

Winter
& the sky
Smears its pasty gray
Across the red bricks
Until all is a pale blur
Dull as dirty snow
Outside my window

Winter
& my grandmother rubs Vicks
On my paper chest
While the other kids
Race & jump & scream
Between the scattered leaves
Outside my window

Those Gray Throgs Neck Winter Days

Those gray Throgs Neck winter days
Of dry grass hard mud & naked trees

Those whipping winds of winter
Hard rain turned to sleet
Pelting the broken pavement
Beneath quick unsteady feet

Those cold hibernating winters
Of watching neighborhood kids
Play football in the field outside our window
Clouded wet with the sweet salty salsa smells
Of my grandma's cooking

Those days I stayed home
From school with asthma
Crawling down from the hard piss-stained smells
Of a thin top bunk mattress to watch *Sesame Street*,
Game shows or early morning sitcoms
The comfort of that projects heat full blast
& burning like a stereo

Those days I waited wheezing & clogged
With phlegm for my old man or uncle
To come & take me to the hospital
For my round of apple juice & epinephrine shots
For my round of spitting up what was sitting
On my lungs, causing my neck to swell
& strain with veins & my eyes to pop out
Wide with suffering

Those days that quickly melted & sank into
The quick dark of daylight saving time
& fights with my cousins, home from school,
For the remote & TV

Those nights I stayed up late with grandma
Watching over me, listening for my wheezing
While she did her crossword puzzles,
Laughing at me laughing at Johnny Carson
Those nights we watched late night
Black & white movies while everyone else
Was asleep

As a Kid I Slept on the Top Bunk

As a kid I slept on the top bunk
On a mattress so thin my midnight
Urine drenched my cousin
As he slept in the bunk below.

Each night I'd be off
In a dream somewhere
&, like clockwork, pee
Would just leak out of me

Like air from a tire or
Water from your ear
After a swim or shower,
The warm calm wetness
Crawling through the mattress
Raining on my cousin's sleeping face.

If my late night deposits
Weren't enough to arouse me
From my sleep, my cousin
Would with his violent kicks to the
Top bunk, complaining to
The entire family about me
Wetting the bed again.

I wet the bed so often my mattress
Was as hard as a dried-out scouring pad
& though I loved sleeping on the top
Bunk, aloft in a nest or a cocoon
Wrapped in the smells & dreams
Of my own creation, it sure didn't
Seem to like me.

For when I wasn't peeing
On my cousin's face,
Turning my mattress into a
Soggy cracker, I was rolling
Off of it, cracking my hard skull

Against even harder black tiles.
Each morning I'd wake
In my wet sheets and
Fruit of the Looms with
Fat puffy eyes
& a head swollen as a
Bowling ball.

Second Grade

I fell for Michelle, a cocoa butter
China doll with a flat chocolate chip face
& hair pulled back so tight she could
Barely keep her eyes open.

We sat next to one another from the first day of school.
I'd assault her with a bouquet of candy & kisses
While she pelted me with a barrage of farts
That torpedoed through her burgundy nylon pants,

Then pointed to me as if I did it.
We'd hold hands under our desks or in line
Where we'd form in size-place order—
She in front of me as I'd kiss her

On the cheek & pass her some candy.
She would turn & smile, then let loose a
Loud one, pointing to me, as the rest
Of the class laughed & shrieked in horror.

Sunday Morning

Café con leche
From a Bustello can

Pan con mantequilla
(Bread with butter)

Scrambled eggs
With ketchup

Bacon fried to a crisp
Potted plants soaking up
The sun

Linoleum lips peeled back
By sneakers and gum

My grandma at the stove
Calling my name

When I Was a Kid

Me & my cousins
Hid under the kitchen table

While my grandmother cooked dinner,
Mashing salt garlic cloves & black pepper

With the *pilón* she brought with her on the plane
As a young woman from Puerto Rico.

An old beat-up black & white TV
With aluminum foil wire hangers for antennas

Provided background music while my aunt
Sat at the other end of the table talking to

My grandmother about the office gossip
At the Ma Bell building at Westchester Square.

My grandmother relished in the names my aunt
Tossed around as if listening to someone explain

The storyline of a soap opera. Eventually our tiny
Throgs Neck Housing Projects kitchen with

The washing machine & spider plants, with
Bustello coffee cans for pots, would fill up

With my aunts & uncles who told stories
In Technicolor Spanglish about growing up

In Spanish Harlem & the South Bronx.
Me & my cousins would make-believe

We were not under the table, trying to keep
From laughing as we strained our ears to translate

The wild salacious stories that had my grandmother
Laughing & laughing as she pounded

Her ancient pestle into the brown worn mortar
That seasoned our lives.

My Grandmother Had One Good Coat

A black wool one with black buttons
Shiny as patent leather shoes
And a smooth furry collar
Just as black

She wore this only
To the doctor or to church

One late afternoon
I came home from school feeling sorry
For an old woman living beneath the
Elevated train below the station
Who sat taunting passersby
On their way to work and to school

She sat coatless on a cardboard box
Hiding her pain
Behind curses and scowls

She could have been
My own grandmother

And the thought of my own
Grandmother homeless
In the cold with no place
To pray and be warm
Made me sad and depressed

When she asked me what was wrong
And I told her without hesitation
She went into the closet
And handed me her black dress coat
And said here put it in a shopping
Bag you'll find one in the broom closet
I don't use it that much anyway

Childhood in the Projects
Is a Fashion Show Nightmare

Where poor kids brag about the clothes they wear
And snap on those that are not up on the latest gear.

Growing up in the '70s, Pro-Keds, Converse,
Adidas and Pumas reigned supreme. You wouldn't be
Caught dead with anything other than what was un-
Spoken and said to be down by law.

The first present I ever got for Christmas
From someone on my long-lost mother's
Side of the family, her sister, my aunt,
A stranger to me, was a pair of orange sneakers—

Not ProKeds, Converse, Adidas or Pumas, but
Big, chunky orange kicks that looked like they had heels
And glowed in the dark!

At that age I wasn't trained in the art
Of graciously accepting a gift I hated,
But, with my instincts in full gear, and an

Arrow between my ears, I smiled and thanked
This stranger, my aunt, and acted as if I loved the present.

Once, out of guilt, I wore them to school
And, it seemed, the entire school: students,
Teachers, principal and all, were watching me
As I clopped my way to class.

It was a nightmare, everything was silent, except for
The clodhoppers wrapped around my feet.

Then the silence was broken by a student
Who burst out laughing, nearly busting a gut
At my expense.

I turned red and hot as a jalapeño pepper,
Tried to play it off like my sneakers
Were the shit, but to no avail.

I went to bed that night with the scoffs and
Wisecracks and jeers ringing in my ears.

After that, I never wore them again.
They remained in the box

In a closet somewhere
For God knows how many years.

Till this day, I can't remember
What ever happened to those sneakers,
And why I always lied when my mother asked
How I liked my present.

TONY MEDINA

I Spent the First Years of My Life in the Arms of Firemen

I spent the first years of my life
In the arms of firemen,
Drawer-less with a T-shirt
And no shoes, watching flames
Lick their way out our
Windows, neighbors gawking
At the wild late night
Entertainment usually
Reserved for the evening
News, children climbing
Onto fire trucks like a
Sandlot jungle gym never found
In their park-less South Bronx slum.
Firemen carrying me through
Railroad flats of smoke and flame
Down narrow flights of rickety
Stairs where kids and teenagers
Kissed and pants rubbed
After school or during daytime
Hooky hours where no one
Was around except construction
Workers and mailmen.
I spent my first few years
Going from apartment
To apartment escaping smoke
And flames ignited by uncles
Who fell asleep drunk and
High with cigarettes dangling
From their bottom lips,
Who fell asleep with their
Clothes and shoes on as if they
Knew they'd have to make a
Mad dash to the door while the rest
Of us slept in other rooms, smoke-
Less and secure, wakened by instinct,
Scents and hysterical cries, frantically
Making our way out into curious crowds
Staring up with a strange sense of awe
And pleasure at water hoses and
Ax handles smashing through
Each window, staring up at the
Big flames and black smoke
Smearing toward the sky.

Alfie's

    Early morning bar
Room full of white drunks, their eyes
    Wet & daring, glare
At my father & me—two

    Black spic birds the wind
Blew in—come in from the
    Cold for change of a
Dollar. They turn from their

    Barstools like *Wild Kingdom* lizards in
Time-lapsed photography. Their eyes say,
    Well well well... What do we have here? smile like the
Grins found in the black & white photos

    Of lynchings. My father, unable to undo the
Knot of memory, to return the smile without
    Giving himself away, does not bother to
Speak. Instead he holds a dollar

    Up at the barkeep. Before my father
Could speak, the bartender says,
    We don't give change here.
What the hell are you

    Doing here? is how my
Eight year-old mind imagines he takes it,
    For he rushes me out of there as if the bus is
About to pull up.

    Before my father could
Turn, I narrow my eyes at them,
    Wave my little brown
Fist in the air long

    Enough for my father to
Grab me by my bony
    Arm & yank me out
Of there, as if to say, *What's*

    The matter with you—
Are you crazy?

Autobiography of a Skinny Puerto Rican Kid from the Projects

I used to give shows for the kids on my block in our tiny three-story projects hallway. I'd make my entrance from the side of the staircase by the mailboxes as everyone sat on the stairs, then do my impersonation of Flip Wilson's Geraldine. Everybody on my block was banking on me becoming a big TV and movie star. I was so obsessed with TV and being an actor or comedian my father scrounged up some money and put me in acting school. Each Saturday morning we'd trudge down from The Bronx to Times Square by bus and train to go to acting class. I did so many impersonations and impromptu puppet shows, all the kids and staff were enamored. But since they didn't put me on TV the day I entered acting school, and I began to get too lazy to wake those Saturday mornings, I quit acting school, letting my father, my family and my entire Throgs Neck Housing Projects neighborhood down. Till this day, my cousin Stevie still rides me about it. I met my mother briefly when I was 5 or 6, then again at 8, 9, or 10. My mother showed up again and somebody said, *That's your mother.* I always thought my mother was my grandmother since she took care of me and I naturally called her Ma. I was a terrible son. When my mother would come pick me up for weekends with her in Brooklyn, I'd nag her constantly every time we walked past or entered a store with a torrential monsoon barrage of BUYMETHISBUYMETHATBUYMETHISBUY METHATBUYMEDISBUYMEDATBUYMEBUYMEBUY BUYMEMEME. As she tried her best to make up for lost time. But I was a dumb kid raised on TV commercials who didn't know any better. I sucked my thumb until I was in high school. Had a big old wart on it the size of a Buick. Had to Bugs-Bunny-Road-Runner-Warner-Bros.-cartoon-TNT blast it off with Anbisol before I entered Norman Thomas High School. Till this day I still rock in my sleep. I slept on the top bunk of a room I shared with my cousins Boobie and Stevie. Every night, to no avail, I'd roll off in my sleep and slam into the floor, waking up screaming with everyone crowded in in a state of panic. I would go to school each day looking like The Elephant Man, my head was so swollen. I used to wet the bed so often my family rented me out as a sprinkler system. Each night my cousin Stevie, who slept on the bottom bunk, would catch a torrential rain of piss in the face that poured through my thin mattress out of me in my sleep. Once I woke from the top bunk in the pitch-black of night to see Dracula staring me in the face. I screamed so loud the entire three-story projects was in our room. Since that day, up until I went to high school, I slept with my grandmother, I was so scared of the dark. Every half an hour, I had an asthma attack. My uncles Richie or Raymond would have to rush me to the hospital at all hours of the day or night. I would stay up nights with my grandmother as she rubbed my chest with Vicks VapoRub (which I also ate among other things like shoe polish, paint chips and the edges of newspapers), then when all was calm, she would lambaste me with her Last of The Big Mamas farts, laughing hysterically as I screamed and moaned in exaggerated complaint; she drank ice water all night and did her crossword puzzles while we watched *The Johny Carson Show* and the *Late Show* movie and the *Late Late Show* movie and the *Late Late Late Show* movie. I stayed home from school so often, Miss Feagan, my first grade teacher, who hated me, put an APB out on me. I spent most of my childhood home sick with asthma watching *Sesame Street, The Electric Company, Mr. Rodger's Neighborhood, The Flintstones, Bugs Bunny, The Jetsons, Gilligan's Island, I Dream of Jeannie* and on and on till my cousins came home from school and we fought for control of the TV. When we finally got a set with a remote control, a big floor model my uncle Robert got my grandmother with drug money, we would hide the remote when we left the house to play or go to school. In 5th grade I got obsessed with *Happy Days*, so much so I thought I was The Fonz (before that it was Jerry Lewis).

I used to slick my hair back with my aunt Vilma's Dippity Doo and carry a black comb in my back pocket. An older kid in our building painted "The Fonz" on the back of my denim jacket as I'd walk around during snack time with my collar and thumbs up, jerking my neck, saying, *Ayeeeeee!!* When junior high hit, I'd go to the school dances with my hair blow dried back into a DA with a John Travolta *Saturday Night Fever* three-piece suit, dancing to "Flashlight" and "The Atomic Dog." On our way to the school dance, my friends and I would strut and sing: *Well, you can tell by the way I use my walk, I'm a woman's man, no time to talk…Ah, ha, ha, ha stayin' alive… stayin' alive*

Thanksgiving at Our House

Is the annual gathering
Of the tribe, a roll call

Come together to see
Who shows up.

Throughout the years
We've lost many:

My Grandmother,
The chief, the Last

Of the Big Mamas,
My four uncles:

Richie, Robert, Raymond
& Ralphie, who died

From sleeping on a
Fire escape that collapsed

And now my father, affectionately
Known as Big Tony.

Only the women are left:
Vilma, Rachel & Josie

And my uncle Freddie
Nicknamed Coco, who

At my father's wake, blurted out:
Five down, one to go!

It is hard to think
That seats that were

Once filled with people
Who have occupied

So much space in your mind
Will no longer be, that

The herd is thinning, year
By year, like a tree in fall

Slouching toward the
Gray-brown slant of winter.

TONY MEDINA

Is There Anything in the World Sadder Than

You sobbing in the bathtub the night your
Grandmother died in her light blue robe
Her Last of the Big Mamas flesh

Shrunken down to brown wrinkles & bones
The pacemaker that held her breath together
The white pills beneath her tongue

Varicose veins wrapped around tree trunk thighs
How she dragged her brown *chancletas* across
The peeled linoleum of our kitchen floor

Religiously getting up to make scrambled eggs
& bacon to make Bustello coffee to
Scream the house awake for work & for school

My grandmother loved to wear her *bata* around the house
Loose fitting & faded with its prints & flowers
She loved getting up early to pray at the edge

Of the bed, pray by the window at the kitchen table
She loved her cheap paperback novels & her
Crossword puzzles & Bob Barker & *The Price Is Right,*

Mac Davis & Glen Campbell on the radio,
Soap operas by day & *novellas* at night on Channel 47
& her water with ice

She'd laugh at my endless ridiculous antics, my
Desire to make her smile and say, *Aye Tony,*
No me haga reír (Don't make me laugh),

Letting loose a machine gun barrage of gas
Blasting me out of the room—her beautiful toothless
Smile with her smooth gums the color of Pepto Bismol

How many times she collapsed on the kitchen floor
Her old brown cane unable to support her weight
I dreaded leaving the house for school or work

& then the military for fear there'd be no one there
For fear she'd be all alone for fear I'd show up
& find her laid out in agony

Or I'd get a phone call from Wherever, USA
Only to anticipate the day she would
No longer be there

With her Hail Marys Full of Grace
Wrapped in the warm kitchen smells
Of Spanish coffee & bacon

36

And now you're dead and now you're dead—you fell from
The hospital bed not knowing where you were

And why your body had failed you so
36 and your mind was gone, gone with the

Nod and high of your youth and your homeboys
Times you just wanted to run the streets and make

Money and make money and now you're dead at
36, dead with white hairs on a balding

Head, dead with tattoos you got in the joint,
Tattoos covering half your body, tattoos

Covering the shrinking flesh of your shrinking
Bones, tattoos covering your heart

Dead are the times you spent on the streets hustling,
Worrying your mother half to death, coming

Home all hours of the night, coming home with
A 36" floor model remote control color TV

Dead are the 5 cars you wrecked nodding off
Behind the wheel—who was to know that the needle

Would finally take you out, or did you take
Yourself out, at 36 at 36 at 36

It Is Hard for Me to Think of You

It is hard for me to think of you
Big brown mama of the laughing flesh

With a face without wrinkles
And a road map on your chest

It is hard for me to shrink you
To the size you had become

Half the battle hardly won
The heart is a long-distance runner

Saddled with battery operated aluminum
The wires meshed into one

It's hard for me to watch you
Struggling for each breath

As if air were the soil of a grave
Filling your lungs

TONY MEDINA

I Am Here in the Pathmark among the Cheeses

I am here in the Pathmark among the cheeses
Feeling like a brie, smelling of blue cheese
Thinking about that Abbott & Costello routine
Where the cheese is so strong
Costello nearly has an asthma attack
Every time Abbott opens the freezer

I am here in the Pathmark among the cheeses
Going from Pepper Jack to cheddar
From mild picante to feta
Thinking about my grandmother's toothless smile
How she used to gum Italian bread
Dunked in Bustello coffee

Those mornings she'd climb out
Of her sickbed to fix breakfast
Even though you'd get up extra early
To beat her to it, she'd stubbornly
Insist on cooking it herself
You couldn't keep her out of the kitchen

Even after she had several heart attacks
And was saddled with a pacemaker
Like an old war horse who refuses
To leave the battlefield
After her endless mornings
Of Hail Marys Full of Grace

She'd hobble into the kitchen with her *bastón* (her cane)
On her swollen legs with the varicose veins
Sit in front of the old beat-up
Black & white with the cigarette burns
And wire hanger antenna
Put on some soap opera or game show

Like *The Guiding Light* or *The Price Is Right*,
The smell of bacon and Spanish coffee
In the air, gumming her
Pan con mantequilla, her bread with butter,
Speaking to me in Spanish
And English

As I get ready for school
As I go from cheese to cheese
In this Pathmark
My grandmother calls out to me
In Spanish and English
To get her her heart pills

My Mother Who Gasps for Air

My mother who gasps
For air
As if gulping
Down water

My mother
Who is two pale
Useless lungs
Wrapped in a fading
Nightgown

My mother who gossips
And complains
In English and
Broken Spanish
Wonders about her
Wandering daughter

My mother who is
Five-foot one
Of street tough
And mettle
Confined by
Stiff creaks
And pain

Whose heart is a
Sprinkler
Drowning her soul
With tears

My mother full of
The Holy Communion
Of trackmarks
Slumps in her sagging body
Of bedsores and creases

My mother with frozen bowels
Lungs stiff as dry sponges
And a cough that
Makes her
Crumble

I Mainline Heroin

I mainline heroin
From my mother's womb,
Trackmarked umbilical
Dreams. I long for
The screaming clutch
Of scag crawling
Through my tiny
Veins like razor
Sharp cobwebs.
When they tell her
Push and she says
Kick I'm sure
She's not talking
About me giving
A sign of life
From where I lay
In the white horse
Amniotic float
Too young to nod or
Vomit my tender
Lungs. I am the
Wet ash scar tissue
Of wasted days.
My waking life
Precipitated by nods.

September

Is green
& gray
W/ a hint
Of lemon
Smiles sour
In the sun
Hidden away
Through clouds
& trees
& drawn shades

September is
My mother
W/ crushed
Grape lungs
In the
Wine time
Of her life

Room 102, Bed A

My mother's lungs sag
Like her pale breasts they give up
On her like men have

I am the one here
After all the lost years gone
Like her youth shot up
Through the rude end of needles
Wasted like her collapsed veins

My mother is still a mystery to me
All these decades later when now she needs me
Still can't believe her heroin baby,
Wheezing asthma boy screaming for a fix
From the belly of an incubator,
From South Bronx Simpson Street, grew up to be
What he wanted to be: poet, professor

What dreams did she have that did not last
Before the party and the streets claimed her
Before all the men used and betrayed her
How did she feel when she wasn't even
Allowed to attend her mother's funeral
Trapped behind bars for a fix she couldn't kick
Strapped with broken daughter born behind that pain

Now she sits in another cold ward
With a third of her lungs left
With oxygen tubes wheelchair and diapers
All that aimless running got her here
With a bum heart and sore bones
With short breath high blood and sugar
And a mind clouded with faded memory

As she gasps for air
She's the one incubated
Now at seventy-
Three and me with no way to
Try and make it all better

No jones coming down
No fix to fix in a hurry
I'm going nowhere

TONY MEDINA

Feeding My Mother at Seventy-two

My mother, half between dreamland and nodding,
Half refuses the insistent prodding
Of hand and fork and all-too bland food, feeding
Her half-baked lies and desperate pleading;

Each triumphant swallow brings me back to days
She missed having abandoned me at birth in a drug haze;
It is my father's mother's hand I remember
Feeding my asthmatic wheeze at two or three,
As I feed her thirty-some-odd years later,

Bent between the gasping glazed guilt of a nod and dream;
As the nursing room window clouds with steam,
My vain words vanish like finger-scrawled letters,
You have to eat so you can get better.

Arrival

Steroids turn my mother's hair from black to white
In less than a year. My mother's family would have

Loved for that to happen to the skin my sister
Inherited from her father, an anonymous black doctor/donor

From Baltimore my mother got with to feed her fix.
My sister's voice and my mother's

Colliding in my head as I think about the July day
I picked my mother up at Reagan National.

She left her common law husband after thirty years.
He'd leave her home tied to an oxygen tank and

Go off to Puerto Rico and take up with another
Woman who could cook and clean and cater to his needs.

Everything my mother did for him—and work at Walmart
And clean office buildings on the side, where she thinks

She got pulmonary fibrosis inhaling chemicals for
Twenty years, scarring her lung tissue into dry sponges.

He kept pushing her to sign away her half of their house.
A broke-down aging narcissist finally met his match;

He must've forgotten that she was street smart
And he, a compromise with her ego;

How a woman settles for a man out of some survival instinct.
I can't believe I allowed this man to keep me from

My daughter for all these years, she tells me.
You lost a lot of time, I say, trying to return my sister's favor

And bring *them* back together.
Curbside at US Airways' arrivals terminal my mother's

In a wheelchair looking tired and helpless, an airline
Oxygen tank strapped to the back of the wheelchair. She's in a

White and blue flower print blouse and navy knit slacks and the
White shoes of someone that lives on an island near water and sun.

I hand her a yellow bouquet and a green oxygen tank to
Add to her Great Escape curbside wheelchair portraiture.

Within a week she is in the ICU at Bethesda General
Holding the hand of a dying woman twenty years her senior,

Assuring her *everything is going to be fine, just fine.*
Her life continuing to be a Fellini film even as it

Rolls on to the credits and the word *finis.*
Months later I'm wheeling her around the mall, the

Rehab center's wheelchair giving my forty year-old back
A first-time golfer's workout. The nurse on graveyard shift,

Who pumps her full of steroids and late night diabetic snacks,
Says to me, *She's gained a few pounds.* I want to say, *No shit.*

Instead I say, *Yeah—and her hair is getting whiter.*
I'm taking her out on the town to get her hair cut and nails done,

Then a rare picture together and then a late lunch— all the shrimp
I'm allergic to she can eat. I'm toasting her girl's night out

With a glass of red wine and in the middle of our dinner,
Her oxygen tank runs out. I'm off to the parking lot,

Trying not to panic.
I come running back to the table with the second one,

Trying to figure out how to work the valve.
Somehow the gods have aligned themselves

On this sunny September Saturday afternoon—
I used to work at a hospital, the waiter says,

Teaching me the righty tighty left loosey routine,
My mother's breathing never skipping a beat.

In a couple of months we will sit down and have our first Thanksgiving
Together where she will tear up the duck unlike an old woman with a

Bad heart diabetes kidney problems bronchitis and a third of her lung capacity.
But she paces herself and the burning logs on the fireplace light up her face.

She finally tells me what happened the night she gave birth to me; how the
Doctor was without answers to why I was so sick, screaming uncontrollably

From the womb of an incubator. *I finally broke down and told him I was on drugs,*
She says. *I was scared—but I had to tell him. I didn't want anything to happen to my*

Beautiful baby boy. Relieved, the doctor turns and tells her, *Thank you, Ms. Gonzalez—*
You just saved your son's life.

The First and Only Thanksgiving with My Mother

I look at her sitting there
In the middle of the crowded inn,

Fireplace roaring, people chattering.
She looks good to me, my mother

An ocean of lost years between us
Comes rushing back as I examine

Her white head of hair for traces
Of black and notice new hair

On her chin where once they
Did not appear

She is proud of me—amazed
That I made it through such

Precarious beginnings
Your grandmother

Would be so proud of you,
She says, referring to my

Father's mother
Every now and then

She tries to hook me up
With one of the nurses,

Bragging about my accomplishments—
My son is a professor…he writes books

She tells me how she used to
Write poetry when she was younger

And pieces of her life begin to
Fit into the puzzle that is us

And I wonder how it is that
She got so lost in a labyrinth

Of pain—how it must have been
Between her and her mother

Forty years later she is feeling at home with
Her son on our first Thanksgiving together

The Old Testament

Why is it so hard to tell the truth about ourselves
Ripping our lives apart with the scalpel of memory
What is it to be laid out on an examining table
Like an auction block to be picked away
Bit by bit, the hard soft scab of secrecy
Who really cares that your mother was on scag
That she left you in the hospital room
Hours after you left her womb
That your pops ran hero'n, got stabbed
In the joint on a seven year bid,
The scar creasing the surface of his lung
What does it matter that you sucked
Your thumb and wet the bed that you
Rocked yourself to sleep and loved the
Smell of airplane glue, that you used to
Sleepwalk and were afraid of the dark
That your chest is caved in and asthma
Wracked your lungs, that as a child you ate
Paint chips from South Bronx walls, ate
Shoe polish and the edges of the *Daily News*
That your uncles sold dope and went to prison
And half your family never graduated from high school
That your grandmother prayed each morning and night
For her nine children and her children's children
That she raised all of us in a handful of rooms
That she kept the family together, though
Her second oldest son died when he
Fell asleep on a fire escape
That collapsed in the Harlem heat
Of her summer sorrows
That her three youngest sons died of AIDS
That she collapsed several times cooking breakfast
With her bad heart, with her pacemaker
With her diabetic legs and arthritis in her hands
And fought for you when the State
Wanted to auction you off at birth
To a white couple from Queens
Why is it so hard to tell the truth
About ourselves

About the Author

Tony Medina was born in the South Bronx and raised in the Throgs Neck Housing Projects. He served in the United States Army and earned a BA in English at Baruch College, CUNY, on the GI Bill. He has taught at Long Island University's Brooklyn campus and Borough of Manhattan Community College, CUNY. The author of several books for adults and children, his poetry, fiction and essays appear in over forty anthologies. Medina, whose most recent book is *I and I, Bob Marley*, earned an MA and PhD in English from Binghamton University, SUNY, and is Associate Professor of Creative Writing at Howard University.

www.ingramcontent.com/pod-product-compliance
Lightning Source LLC
LaVergne TN
LVHW011426080426
835512LV00005B/298